Mayeena R

CW00431016

Sunsets

of the

Soul

Sunsets Of The Soul

Sunsets of the Soul

A Poetic Memoir

By Mayeena Rose

Sunsets Of The Soul

Mayeena Rose

ISBN: 9798673426128

Contact and business enquiries: mayeena.rose@gmail.com

For

My son, my Prince. You are my light. It is hard for me to find words that carry enough depth to fully explain what you mean to me. "Thank you, I love you" will never fully translate the feeling of love and gratitude I feel for you. You are such an amazing human being. Thank you for all that you are, and most importantly for your patience and your supportive interest during the writing process of this book. I remember when you asked me : "So, you want to become a poet when you grow up?", and the answer was "eerrmm...yes", I'm still growing up, every day, but yeah, I'm following my dreams baby ! Thank you for believing in your Mom!

My mother, thank you for being my biggest supporter. You allowed me to be free and you have never censored my truth. Thank you for everything.

My father, thank you for transmitting your love for literature to me and for always supporting me.

My brothers and sisters, you've been a driving force in this project. You are the best team I could ever ask for. Thank you so much!

Murphy, thank you for the way you take care of my heart, and the way you make me feel safe in love while I follow my dreams. Thank you for giving me something joyful to write about.

Inene, Holly, Melannie, Hami, Prisca, Gwendoline, Celine, who have been sources of support and motivation.

On a final note, I want to thank God for keeping that flame alive in me. Thank you for your Guidance and that little push that helped me to cross the rivers of self-doubt to reach the land of self-realisation.

Table of content

Mayeena Rose

PREFACE

Sunsets are so soothing and appeasing to me. A beautiful symphony of colours at the end of the day for an attentive eye.

To me, sunsets give a calming sense of achievement: you've made it through the day. A feeling of awe and a sense that life is, at times, an enmeshment of light, hope, beauty and mystery, and that it would be foolish for us to think we can master or find the answers to everything.

The displays of colours during sunset also remind me of the concept of "transition". And, aren't we all too familiar with this concept? Our lives are a succession of transitions, taking place in our careers, our personal lives, our minds, our bodies and our spirits.

I hold the intimate feeling that sunsets not only represent a transition, between light and obscurity, but it also echoes the duality of my being, oscillating between faith and fear, trauma and healing.

That is probably the reason why the sunset is my favourite time of the day to reflect, to pray, to focus, to pause, to simply enjoy the moment.

This is also the moment where, strangely enough, my mind gets creative and my heart wants to speak to me.

Hence this collection of poems. In this poetic memoir, I composed music with the words to details different key moments in my life, the most defining transitions. The words stemmed and poured from moments, difficult or agreeable, of reflection or introspection. Writing has been a difficult process at times, but more so, a liberating and therapeutic process.

Thank you for embarking on this journey with me. I feel deeply grateful that you have chosen to engage with my words, and with my world. Sit cosily and comfortably. Inhale, Exhale, and enjoy.

With love, always.

Mayeena

Mayeena Rose

CHAPTER 1

DAWN

At dawn, find me musing

About mysteries, new beginnings...

While we all long for brighter hours

I waver to the sway of mysterious tremors,

I should say, really, this life is humbling

Enchanting and mind boggling.

Still, at dawn, you'll find me musing

On all the love I've been missing,

Confiding in God with faith and fervour,

I will sing and pray with candour

About the time that is passing

And the times that we're living.

AURORA

It was a glimpse of Aurora
That I discerned at nightfall
Have faith, believe me, it's true
A dazzling magnetic spark
I couldn't believe such a glow

The same streamers of light
I searched them deep within my soul
But this very gift was my cue
A radiant unpolished aura
Ready to dispel grubby shadows

However, life gets tougher
I wonder, will the light rise for all?
And what am I gonna do?
Maybe design my own life like it's art
I'll paint it magical, chromatic, whimsical

Just like an Aurora

DECEMBER

Shaky, moving Awakening

A life far from pristine

She was a real Queen

Longing to see what life could bring

So here, splendid, was my mother,

At the apex of life's magic

Birthing in the earliest hours

Of a Sunday morning

Just like soft, wintery sunrays

and bouncy, shiny stellar plates

Fire and Passion illuminated

This very special birth day

Our bond was crystallised

Soon as I met your eyes

And I felt the Presence over me

Mercifully grounding my Imani

And like superb Northern Lights

Each birth is a celestial celebration

More wowing than a million

Souls rejoicing during Kwanzaa

ROOTS

Alright

I need a mic check

For this short introduction

That I'm about to pen

My lineage can be traced

Straight to the Motherland

If your mind can paint

Tropical rainforests

Plateaus and plains

An array of landscapes

Harmattans in arid regions

Or grandiose fertile lands

I'll bring to your attention

How my people have thrived

Through the test of time,

Crime and theft

Nevertheless

It's a blessed filiation

A heritage peaking as high

As the tallest, sturdiest baobab

That you could ever find

In my ancestor's realm.

LINEAGE

See

My bloodline carries

A mighty legacy

Kingdom of Ghana

Kingdom of Mali

Lands of gold,

Cocoa

Ivory and coffee

Moonsoons

Lagoons

And high savannas

The warm hues

Of the earth

Maroon

And copper

As a child

In my mind

Dad was a President

He's a legitimate descent

Of the Ghana empire

Sub-Saharan man

With colossal intellect

He transmitted to me

His passion for great stories

and his ancestors' history

A girl from the West

Mom's a true empress

From the *dix-huit-montagnes*

To the Paris of Africa

Riding with her head high

Always deeply spirited

She kept the passion of her prime

From her I carry in my bloodline

An essence so fierce, *fancy* and fine

See

My lineage

Is a rich

polyphony

MAMA (INTERLUDE)

Mama

I know you're crushed

But please tell me

Just how much

You love me

And that you see

In me

All of your dreams.

DEEPDIVING

The sweet fragrance of innocence

Citrus, cinnamon, warm pastries

All added together

Softly embalm my spirit

It all started out so well

Mom and Dad hoped

For fruitful seasons

And promising horizons

Then it went ballistic

Fears strangling like a tight rope

And triggers strafing up bad spells

Soiling our DNA like arsenic

There was no way to foretell

How gigantic and profound

the impact of unhealed

generational wounds

was to be...

So, often, at night

 I dive deep

Into these sunken memories

Of warmth and serenity

Just for a glimpse of candour

Yes

I do remember....

DEATH 1

My memory
Hijacked
Reformatted
Life Hacked.

But the greys
The senses
The place
The blaze,

Intact,
I feel it.

He profaned
The sacred,
My family,
My sanctuary,
My body.

My innocence
Why
Why
Why

Is this life?
My life?

Five
Years
Old

He made
my mind a hell,
Bombshells of pain.
I could never
Live again,
Breathe
The same again.

He killed me
At five
I never was
A child.

Soul bombed
Traumatised
So I
Just died.

Maybe
I'm alive
Or at least I try.

But he killed me,
At five.
I died.
I never was
A child.
And I think
that's what I miss

The most.

BREACH

For years I 've been

Seeking hastily

Comfort

In your words

Solace

In your embrace,

Was it all

In pure vain ?

Did you even notice

That your daughter

Had died?

If you don't mind

Paying attention

You will hear :

She sings

A broken song.

On a burning edge

Torn between love

And resentment,

I never asked you to chose

But to acknowledge

My heart has drowned...

Please hold me for a moment

I can't self- soothe.

I waged this war alone

In abyssal angst,

Erring in bewilderment,

Blown by titanic torments.

I now understand

That forgiveness

Would be a lifelong

Healing process.

NOBODY LIKES WINTER

Nobody likes winter

The burning frost

The sunlight lost.

From afar

The season looms, glacial

Inhospitable,

However,

In winter,

When the sun

Gleams at his furthest,

Is when spirits

Come together

To surmount

And endure.

Observe

How life

Eventually surpasses

This inevitable

Cycle of life :

You will survive.

I too,

Used to dislike winter,

When the weather

Is the coldest

Ever.

So I've learnt

How to enlighten

My own little Home,

How to lend a hand

To a needy neighbour,

And God is my saviour

Now I know

The land of hope

Is never barren .

Mayeena Rose

CHAPTER 2

Mayeena Rose

FOG

Blinding mist
and
Heavy clouds,

Darks alleys
with
Stark stories,

The violent cost
Of
Innocence lost.

Prematurely
Twice
They tried to kill me.

Springing from the hurt
Watch
For my superb rebirth.

ROSES AT WAR

What's going on?
Have I turned
The wrong page?
Can you confirm
The reason
I'm held hostage?

How come
Growing into a woman
Made me feel even more
Vulnerable?

I already learned
As a kid,
five-year-old girl
It's better
To be hidden
Than to be
Seen.

Still I longed
To explore
Love and freedom.

So when
My figure got plumper
My chest grew fuller

My flesh felt softer,

To my greatest horror
I became a prey,
A flustered dove
Bleakly entrapped
In a cluster of bullets.

DEATH 2

Catching the wrong type of attention

At the wrong moment.

At first, I did not pay caution

But he became persistent,

Short days and long afterschool detentions

When we met, it was no accident.

A predator's plan coming to fruition

After weeks and weeks of harassment.

"I know where you live anyway" he mentions

And my fire became hesitant.

I don't ask too many questions,

And he is scary, vehement.

I just suppressed my emotions

And I was dead, just like that, in an instant.

Do you know about consent?

I know and I don't.

AFTERMATH

Staggering through life

Avidly brewing wrath,

The sequel was no surprise.

My heart grew dark

And coarse like coffee.

Feeding off from the cracks

And the voids in my heart,

My grudge was ravaging

Ferocious and greedy .

We tried the medicine

But no amount of detox

Could purge the venom,

No doctor could put an ending

To my infamous aftermath.

ARSONS OF THE SOUL

For sure my body knew desire
But never did my yearnings
Lead me to wage wars
Or to profane sacred spaces.
At the very beginning
Of our Springs,
We arrived
Freshly unprepared
For this enforced warfare.
The following horror stories,
Need a trigger warning.

Suddenly,
Our blooming bodies
Turned into **templates**
For criminal
Rites of passage,
Sites of terror
For illicit practices.

In the end,
We all
Tried to assemble

Our very own arsenal
To deter aggression,
Halt the transgressions.
Our resistance
Took different forms.
Some of us remained and overcame
Some of us are resting in pain.

COLLECTIVE SILENCE

Wounded masculinities

And shadowy father figures

Was the near perfect recipe

For coming-of-age disasters.

It was not much the violence

But more the collective silence,

How many never stood trial

For their silent carnage

And carnal crimes?

BY DEFAULT

Love has been denied to me for so long,

I settled for you whom I couldn't find at home.

Anything of close semblance,

I don't care if it's all pretence.

My request was urgent,

Anything to keep me afloat.

Anything to ground me in the present

We whispered our vows by default

While cries sorrow cut deep in my throat.

Mayeena Rose

THE FIRST RELATIONSHIP

I tried to run away

But where could I stay?

So I jumped right on the ship

Blindfolds and all?

No compass, no draft,

We embarked on a broken craft

With no defined course.

At first

I felt restored a bit,

Then the ship went adrift

Before it all sunk.

LOVE LETTERS

He's sorry
He is
Always
And I stay
In a warped silly
Distorted way
Love is spelled abuse
So love pollutes
My life stream
My most intimate beliefs.

He acts with malice
Slashing
My self esteem
With other girls
With dirty words
And when these swords
Aren't sharp enough
He pens me love letters
With his bare hands
And his fists.

H.IM

I hate thinking of h im
Or should I say
Being reminded of h im
People throwing h is name around
Like fake aphrodisiac bath bombs
Thinking maybe I'm missing
Ex-bae and his abusive ways
It triggers me like a sucker punch
A crazy blow
That's if you care much
To know
It's like an avalanche
The very few remnants
Boxing me
Coaxing me
Back into that dark gloomy room
Drowning
Suffocating
In a sticky stinky
Slimy liquid
Colour murky green,
Or perhaps Navy blue
I don't have a clue
But that sticks like glue
Or maybe chewing gum
Anyways, it drives me mad

Shame, guilt and disgust
It all gets mixed up
And I explode like a soda can
That has been fondly churned
In the end,
Here's how I prepared
my spirit for the win.
I just wrote h is name
On a piece of paper.
And threw it in the bin.

LETTERS FROM STOCKHOLM

The tragedy

Was me believing

That his violence

Was actually

A love language,

A manifestation

Of an intense passion.

I was in pure denial.

When I thought

I was finally healing,

Finally winning,

He ransomed

What was left of me

To feed

His megalomania.

Eventually,

He pitted me

Against my inner child.

The irony of destiny,

I was erroneously in love.

My intuition,

A little broken lamp,

Went astray

Exploring toxic

Unknown lands.

Here I was,

His emotional

Punching ball

Until words

Turned into missiles,

Black eyes and deep blues.

That guy didn't want peace.

I now realise

How my sorrow

Fuelled his bruised ego.

I stayed there

For nearly a thousand

Eight hundred

Twenty something days

'Til I hit rock bottom.

Now I hope you understand

Why you've never

Got to receive

My Letters from Stockholm.

IT'S OVER (INTERLUDE)

Don't want to be harbouring

Harrowing feelings.

I'm preparing

To raise Kings and Queens

And he's unfit.

So I left

And never

Ever

Looked back.

It's over.

DYNAMITE

Is it really gonna help,

All that fury and shame ?

You sprinkled the mixture with pride

What a toxic amalgam.

An alchemist of modern times

But your feels are off the charts

You're now your own dynamite.

Babe, listen, watch out

I want you to shine like a star

But the bigger the commotion

The more spectacular

The explosion

Have you seen these Blue Supergiants ?

They burn and blaze to infinity

But the end can be extraordinary

I know it sounds crazy

You may not be ready

Or willing

Yet.

Take my hand,

Here's the big step :

Learn the science

Behind forgiveness

To let go of the rage.

Find your safe place

Just for the sake

Of your inner child,

I want to see you rise

Way, way up from the ground.

THE FLOWERS OF JUSTICE

There's blood and dust
All over my flowers
They hid their faces
And burned my garden
Of roses, jasmines, and orchids
Timid eyewitnesses
Preferred to look the other way
With their conscience crumbling
In ashes and sand
I could write an encyclopaedia
Or leave a thousand
Blank pages
That could never
Describe the carnage

but I chuckle, how stupid !
I have faith my flowers
will grow again
like primroses in winter
I know to persevere
I've been failed
by the justice of men
but I don't soak in bitterness

I'm cultivating the seeds

Of forgiveness
Raking the debris away
They've been getting in the way
Like unhinged madmen
And my future children
Already resent them
The invasive weeds
But no anger; No hatred,
Their soul is pure, untainted

It's all left to me to heal
To thrive and resist
Happiness and peace
Gently flowering my kids
Into stellar human beings.
That will be my justice.

CHAPTER 3

IT HURTS

Sometimes,

I wake up in pain.

It hurts.

It hurts

The whole

Day.

Some days

I can pinpoint.

Some days

I can't.

I just endure,

I don't want to disturb.

But deep down I'm scared

Of what my body is trying to tell.

Some days it's in my neck,

The nervous connections in my brain,

The headaches and migraines,

At times it's the womb,

Contracting in pain,

My garden burning in flames,

Perplexed, guilt ridden,

Sometimes it's the hear,t

Punching and weeping,

Palpitating,

Or the skin,

The raging eruptions,

Spreading and scorching.

At times,

My immunity

Rebels against me,

And seems to see me

As the big enemy.

Sometimes it's the love I've given,

And that has been forfeited.

Sometimes it's the love that's missing.

It creates infinite rifts.

Past treasons

Traumatic events

Consuming me like poison

And I don't pay attention.

The whole body is scarring...

Am I healing?

Releasing the toxins?

So many directions,

So many dimensions,

I need to evacuate

Open all the doors.

But my body

Won't listen to me.

It wants my attention,

Now it's payback time

For my oversights

And all the occasions

I let my pain

Bulldoze my body

Into oblivion.

It hurts.

It hurts he whole day,

Sharp and dull.

I don't really know what to do

So I just sit and cry

I try to listen more closely

I try to soothe me

I let the wind embrace me

I try to lull the pain

I try to hear the rain

The whims and the wails

And it soothes.

It soothes away.

I try to smile,

I try to sleep,

I try to laugh a little,

I try to love a little more.

Tomorrow's another day.

MEA CULPA

The body
Cried
And cries.
I tried
To silence
And smother
The riots
When it
Really
Needed me
For comfort,
Support.
My tears
Fill
Empty rooms.
In my own
Water
I'm secure
I wash
The wrongs
And soothe
The blues,
Softly.
But still,
I'm clumsy.
The waves

Get heavy
It smashes
And squashes
Inside of me.
I still cry
Sometimes.
But now
I Believe.
And I know
How to swim.
Full of trauma
Within
But
I love you.
Body.
We are
Healing.

Thank you
For carrying me,
Fighting for me,
And for reminding me
Of my history.

CHORUS

You address me with urgency

With a sweet cacophony.

Wee hours or evenings,

You want to talk to me.

It's such an eerie sensation

When we're in dissonance...

I'm willing to make amends.

After all,

It's on you I depend,

You, my heart.

Just teach me the chords,

And I'll learn all the words

Or I'll co-write the lyrics.

I'll dance to your beat.

Now I'm listening,

It's loud and clear,

Your laments are valid.

I'll pay attention

To your torments.

Heartbreaks and grief

Made you so weary,

But you have to promise

No more beating me

To the ground.

Let's agree,

On a new song.

Let me join you

In harmony,

There is

A refined melisma

That I want to sing,

For you my heart.

TRAUMA

Pain and trauma come in layers
Made me question my stance
As a believer
I did redouble in prayers
And tried my best
Took so many wrong turns
Before realising
The box was empty
I've left it here to burn
I've left it here to turn
Into a sour, vagabond soul
Longing for healing

All I need is more time
More space
I need to reconnect
With my Father in Heaven
And a sit in my mother's garden
So we both can rest
So we can both sunbathe
Make amends
Hold each other
Again
Heal the wounds
With soothing sounds
Uproot deep, shaking truths
And put our fears to the ground

Our past is our greatest hurdle
But now I'm with you Mama
Here's to our virtuous circle
Here's to transformation beyond trauma.

THE CAGED BIRD

To break free from the cage

I had to release the rage

Deliberately

I could've burnt all the sage

I wouldn't have reached this stage

Presently

If I hadn't gripped the courage

To lay my pain on these pages

Truthfully

So I sang and swoon, plunged from the edge

The fall was dreadful, leastways I'm no longer hostage.

Mayeena Rose

LET ME BE

I'm tired

Of having

To justify

My healing,

My rationale

For existing.

Tired

To cover

Crimes

And lies

I did not

Commit.

Let me

Be.

Let me

Breathe.

And please,

Close the door behind you.

Mayeena Rose

THE WORD BOX

I try to be

Deliberately free,

Sans artifice

And authentic

With my pen,

To ensure

The words

Are floating

From me,

No boxing

No forcing

No forging

To fit

Me

Or

My story.

TOMORROW

I was feeling so scared

Innately unprepared,

But one night,

I said let's go!

Dance, sing, scream,

Chase and catch your dreams!

Love out loud, and laugh

Before the candle dims out.

Don't put your life off

To tomorrow.

BLANK PAGES

Writing

Is

To heal

The crisis

 Of my spirit.

My quill

Seldom is brisk,

It's rather fleeing

And faltering.

Still,

Blank pages

Always

Entice me

To explore,

To bleed out

The trauma.

I'm riddled with self-doubt,

Yet even if it takes

A thousand messy drafts

To perfect my craft,

It doesn't matter to me

I'm happy.

Writing

is

A catharsis

Creativity

Is my therapy.

This is my art, my truth

And my way-out.

SKETCHES

I've tried to sketch

The path of my destiny.

Inevitably,

You put me to the test.

In veracity,

Intimately,

I long to please You

So allow me

To pen my truth,

Please.

Give me your Blessing.

I know

It's Your Whisper

I feel

At my core.

A gentle,

Warm candle

Burning evermore.

Great Edifier,

Supercharge

My ink

And my spirit

So I can flourish.

Great Alchemist

Thank you

For propelling

My foaming thoughts

Into

Kaleidoscopic

Weaves of words

To heal my wounds.

CHAPTER 4

UNPROTECTED

I have been,
We have been
Feeling unprotected,
Utterly neglected.
Threats everywhere
and they say in war all is fair.
Exposed to users, imposters
abusers, scavengers,
Family ties
Abruptly severed
By heavily silences
And dark secrets,
Violence and regrets

I slowly, surely built myself
A glowing armour of shame
Proudly equipped
With a devouring fear
I couldn't tame.
A little girl in the battlefield
I earned badges and scars
That seem so unreal.

Where to find solace?
Where is that place,

Where I'm free and safe,
Where at least, I can rest?

A BASKET OF STRANGE FRUITS

The medias
Have been feeding me
A basket full
Of strange fruits
Lately
What's that type of show
Powered by grief and sorrow?
How far can you go
For a follow
Or a top place
On the explore page?
If you don't mind me
Asking
Do you salivate
When you see
Real death
Black death
All over your screen?

TRIGGER WARNING

My words here

Won't make justice

To the plethora of feelings

We've been facing

And the unknown stories

Awaiting justice

But surely

Mediatising black death

Can't be the cure

Me, my sister

And my brother

Here, smothered and pestered

By aggravating algorithms

That send us flying

To the extreme

Numb, rife, desensitised.

Do have an idea

Of what we endure?

Don't be a voyeuristic

Bystander

You're reviving

Centuries of trauma

At a cellular level,

Reactivated

To the trigger

Of a trend

Or a like.

THE TRAP (INTERLUDE)

I've been angry

For so long

My tank is running out...

Talk about a drought .

All I can do now is thrive

Before I fall into

The trap.

WRONG CASTING

I was made to think
I was a victim,
Perpetually
Because of my skin colour,
My past,
My gender,
The mosaic
Of my identity,
And the cracks
In my story.

An underdog
A statistic
And a mule.

Made to normalise the anguish
As normal and systemic,
Sorrow
Inscribed at the core
Of my synopsis,
Of my existence,
Insidiously.
But see
My life's not a movie,
Not a reality show.

I don't exist
For your entertainment.

Oh,
I was fooled
to even believe
For a while.
Now see me beam
And laugh
At the truth.
Didn't you know?
I'm actually
Free, Bombastic
Gracious, delicious
Bright, light
And Supersonic
Both deep and sweet,
Soft and strong,
Powerful and precious.
I have a choice,
you should rejoice!
I am my main act
As a matter of fact
I'm my scenarist
and my director.
I am, oh, so loved

A creation of God
Didn't you know?

There's no price
To my self-agency
Just get me out
Of that cast.

A BIT OF NEL, A BIT OF SULA

In me,

A little bit of Sula

A little bit of Nel.

Didn't know what to do with my pain

Then, of course

I became dangerous.

So I turned ache into art

And upheld my worth.

Armed with a pen,

From this moment forth

I want my own say

In the making of myself.

SPACE (INTERLUDE)

Sis,

I know

It gets tough,

But there enough

Room and space

In the universe

For our spirits

To coexist.

Just know :

We got this.

STARS

What a Journey
And to think
It's just starting...
Can you get a grasp
Of what it takes ?

Here's a bit more of my story
In each page
Hidden behind the words
Or intertwined with my prose
You trace the fragrance
The influence
Of every woman
Every meaningful encounter
That helped me stand taller

I have stumbled
Lost a few battles
I had to self-dismantle
To learn to live again
Thank God I met some Stars
Along the way
Radiating from their core
Coated in beautiful layers
And they rocked my universe

Graciously they agreed
To bathe me
With some of their light
Patiently they agreed
To share with me
Stirring stories and fruitful tales

With some, I shared a few pages
With other, full chapters
With most, I listened
And payed homage
With many, we rejoiced
We laugh and fought

I found robust and soft shoulders
Where I could lay my head
And unravel the knots in my chest

You
My sisters
My mothers
Inspiring figures
My best supporters
Glass ceiling shatterers
Students, nurses, youth mentors
Hairdressers, hustlers, doctors
Activists, rappers, designers,
Bossbabes, housewives, teachers,

Engineers, shopkeepers, mothers
Single mothers, survivors, trailblazers.

Now
Do you get
What it takes?
It takes a village
It takes a community
It takes a tribe
It takes some time
It takes an allyship
It takes a friendship.

It takes a blue sky
Full of loving stars.

THE ROAD IS LONG

Sis, just hold on,

The road is long

Steep and sharp,

Plus, our shoes are

Already worn out.

Maybe we can learn to fly,

Maybe we can break free,

Chose our trajectory?

Let's go for it

And when your baggage gets too heavy

I'll help you to carry it,

Benevolently,

Just like you helped me carry mine

You did pull up for me

So many times...

This is an ode to you my Sister,

And to all my Sisters.

In blood or in spirit.

The souls I like to keep

Real close to me,

Floodlights of love.

She's a warm lighthouse

When the night gets deep.

Even scattered around Earth

We endeavour

To be there for each other.

Sister,

Sisterfriend,

I got your back,

You're exceptional.

I see you and I value you.

I honour you and I need you.

Most importantly, I do love you.

YOU DON'T SEE COLOUR

When you say
You don't see colour
You're erasing
My experiences
You're dismissing
My struggles
You're silencing
My story
You're pillaging
My richness
Take a stand
And acknowledge
My melanin
Don't fret
Take me in
It's a shame
Fear refrains
You from valuing
The wider scope,
And all beautiful shades
Of life's kaleidoscope

PUT BROWN ON THE PODIUM

You were wrong to think

My skin colour was a risk

Perhaps you're intimidated

By these glorious shades?

Here we celebrate

All skin tones

In all their glory,

The whole spectrum.

Let's flip the story

Unravel the status quo

Demonopolize the space

And put Brown on the podium

For once and for all

Time to show some skin

Caramel, Dark plum

Chestnut or red brown

Creamy, or light cinnamon

The lustre of copper

Gold and mahogany

We bring out

A thousand shades of brown

And through the night I still shine

My shade goes deep like red wine

I won't waste a ray of light

For idiotic remarks

I like my pigment

Healthy and intense

Black is beautiful

You're the one who's been fooled

I celebrate my skin tone

I own it

I love it

That melanin is honeying

All that richness inside of me

DEEP BURGUNDY

May, belle and rebelle

Keep all your pastels

I crave the sparks

And I like my red

Deep and dark

I stand

Between rose ebony

And mahogany

With shades of Razzmatazz

These are my home colours

You'll have to be

A bit more exact

Cause I'm everything

I keep it real and clean

No time for counterfeits

I'm not fond of the bland

Not fond of bleak

Let the richness expand

Let it leak

Give me intensity

Give me deep burgundy.

A BLACK WOMAN

I am
A Woman
And I'm Black

I'm strong, often
And I fall, sometimes.
Because I am Human.
My essence's too rich to define.
They want me to live in chains
And to cover up dark crimes...
But what about my pain?
When is my time to shine?

I am
Black
And I'm a woman

But can you see beyond my flesh?
Can you taste my uniqueness?
I need sweet words and less trouble
And a room I can call my own.
A queen: delicate, formidable;
My hair a curly, ornate crown.
My incense is of orchid and rose,
I'll lull you into love in my alcove.

I am a Black Woman

Blooming, with or without lovers
The energy of a million sunflowers.
I need the sun, I need the fun,
I need to hum, beating my own drum.
Love...Love is here, on the horizon
Hence my soul repelling your poison.
I'm one among billions.
And one in a million.

I am.

CHAPTER 5

VENUSIAN

For long I assumed

I was just a fervent lover

Seeking someone that could

Douse my fires

Though in truth

The someones mostly bow

To the pressure

My heart is guarded and fiery

Leaving both of us suffocating

Under the heavy weight of memories

And moods fusing, erratic and volcanic

Babe, don't call me extreme

Sometimes I'm just muddling

In the grand scheme of things

I've been used to indulge

In hot water,

I now feel the urge

To let off some steam.

Lord, allow him

To cool me down,

I don't wanna be

His deadly twin,

I won't let him drown.

Use him

To show me

What love can be.

FEEL IN

I can't mute

I can't dilute

My feelings

For you King

It's electrifying

And at the same time

So, so appeasing

I find it crazy

How you sweeten my life

And soften my heart

I want you for real

And I'm all in

Like, head over heels

I'll honour my part

Of our tender deal

And I'll give you

Something real

Something

That has no price

All organic

No aspartame

YOU, YOU, YOU

On you I feen
Tell me what's a queen
To do ?

Pure like Jasmines
My love always wins
For you

Fantasising
Yearning to be seen
By you

Yang with the Yin
And both hearts fusing
See, boo?

Booming, braving
Wait 'til this dream
Comes true.

NU SOUL

I want to believe

what she said, Jill

that you love me

confidently

in my entirety

I needed tuition

To efface

a deeply ingrained

 miseducation

to amend

my trajectory

before

the grand finale

You proved the most

And I honed my worth

It's a real woman's work

But let me show you more
More of what we deserve

If you wish
For you, I'll sing
The perfect picture
Me, you, us
vibing under the moon
harmonising and humming
divinely attuned

empty pledges of forevers
often turn bitter
but you will never, ever
be a non-factor
if I sing for you
I'll sing in truth
I'll make it nice, sweet and fun
through the riffs and run
babe, it doesn't have to hurt

So love me

Confidently

in my entirety

Nut never

Equivocally

STAY (INTERLUDE)

It was a crazy year for sure

But you met me halfway

And your days were brighter

So I prayed you'd let me stay

Could be a day

Or a year....

I'm sure life won't hurt

As long as we're together

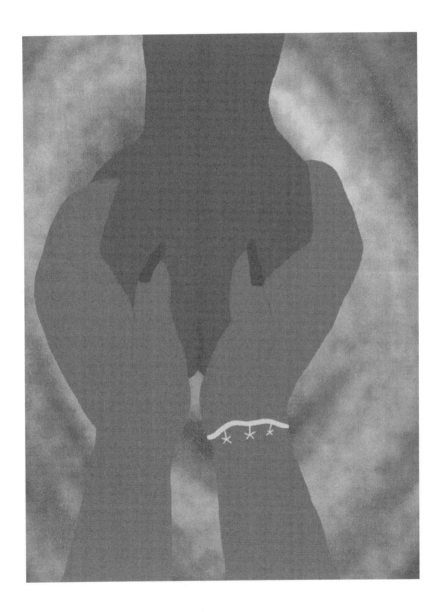

INTIMATE

Can you
Help me
Make it right?

I'll show you
Where it aches

Can you speak
To my body
Touch it
Gently

Whisper
To her
Tell her
Sweet words

It's gotta be real
Don't pretend
Don't offend
Can you be
A friend
Allow me to feel

She's been through wars
Now can you

Accept the scars?

SAFE LOVE

I woke up

Dreaming

Drifting

All jazzed up

Reminiscing about our groove

Mind full of flashes of you

You were just a fantasy

A pure imaginary

Then I realised you were real

And that you were here

So I let my heart breathe

Took of the armour

And waited in stupor

You told me "baby don't hide

Don't dim your colours

Your views about love"

And you did not shoot

You accepted my word

You cherished my truth

You took all of me

And you did not kill me.

MOONS AND SEAS

We go
With the flow
Unaware of surroundings
I set the tone and you tame the pace
Moving me into these interstellar places
With purple hues, filled up with passion and haze

I embark on the journey
Swaying from side to side
To the high and the lows of your tides
Riding your waves, slowly, smoothly
I know where I'm heading
I won't deviate

I pull upon you
And you push my water
I'm not trying steer the ship
I trust you with us
I won't desist

There will be
Storms and typhoons
But together we can cope
And whenever you lose sight of hope
I am your Northern Star
If you drift afar

I make you
Come to me
With the power
Of a thousand moons

THE MOONS OF JUPITER (INTERLUDE)

I pray that our chapters

Together

Surpass in numbers

All of the moons

Of Jupiter

Mayeena Rose

PILLOW TALK

I want to talk with you, King

I mean...

I got you under my skin...

Most times

I don't know how to speak

My feelings

I'm still learning

Though I could draw my love

In colours

I could show I care

With poems

You

You know how to talk

Like a real man...

And I like how you talk

With your hands

But not that way ...

Your touch is soft

Never harming

It doesn't hurt

At least not like....

Never mind...

I guess I'm trying to say

You make it easy to love

I don't feel hostage

I thank you

Cause with you

I'm never scared.

LIGHT YOU UP
(INTERLUDE)

If you allow me

I'll light you up

From within

I will blaze into your sky

Like Venus

On a summery night

THE VELVET OF THE NIGHT

In the velvet of the night
Is when I question my plight,
My sweet baby
Stargazing at me
And I imagine
A galaxy
Of possibilities
Maybe
We can heal
Our miseries
And compromise
Love's demise
Join me in spirituality.
And let us seek mercy
You and I
Singing hopeful litanies
Aloud or in heart
Warmly, softly
Like arising rays of light
After velvet of the night.

CHAPTER 6

2018

Can you come over
Just for a minute?
It'll be quick...
I think we need to talk...

Perfect opening for a thriller
Or a dispute.

What was the issue?
I don't remember...

Ticking clocks
Bad coping skills
If you don't
somebody else will

Now, "us" becomes a problem
And this is a storm I can't tame.
And...damn... I wasn't prepared...
But who can I blame?

I was hot, cold,
In love and in lust.
You were loyal,
but I *don't know how to trust.*

Wait...

You don't want to hurt me
So you hide the words within.
I read it in your face
And flew off in flakes,
Standing at the brink
Of an heartquake....

And like that, I'm left with
All the love I couldn't give,
Piling up over my heart
Like a massive weight...
I damn near broke
The Richter scale...

I didn't expect us to break,
I really think
Our together was great...

I try to find the words
In English
But they are slippery

My love is muffled
By the tears

It's messy...

But you stay here
Waiting for me
To fall asleep

It was the first time
You saw me crying...
Remember that night
Of two thousand eighteen?

NUPTIAL BLISS

That wasn't lust, that wasn't rush.
I was not trying
To save face.
I just
Wanted to be queen
In a white dress.

I was
A bit too scared
Of this boomerang nightmare:
Childhood lies,
And cunning fairy tales
That blossom into hells

Honestly
This is the future I could see
A beautiful yet complex synergy.
Yes, it's true
I wanted my groom
To be you.

HYPHENATE
(INTERLUDE)

We share

The first letter

Of our first name

When is the time when

You give me your last name ?

I'll borrow it from time to time

Even though in reality, it would be mine.

Let me think and see if I want to hyphenate

You can be in charge of picking the wedding cake.

GROOVOSOLO

My heart

Is enmeshed

And moving

To the rhythm

Of your moods.

Fluctuating

In a brisk swing.

Just like the wind.

Let these

Warm easterlies

Gently twine

Our worlds,

Love.

Then plunge

Into the ocean

With passion.

Sans parsimony.

Don't taste me

In chunks.

Savour all

Of my charms.

We're both

Gathered here

for the matrimony

Of our souls.

NO CLOSURE

You're tiptoeing
Around romance
And deep diving
Into my essence

We made up our minds
Twenty-seven times

I'm the past
In your present
No sign of closure
In the near future

NEPTUNE

Yes

A thousand things could go wrong

And there's a million ways to make it right

Don't wilt in my winds and storms

I'm working on me Love, I promise

Still scorching at the core

I'm now starting to cool down

My clouds look intensely bright

Crystal-like and sparkling

No

I'm not after mountains of gold

Rivers of pebbles and jewels

Your self is what keeps me warm

Baby you are my stronghold

Lay there, laze into my deep seas

And nudge in, my ocean is like Neptune

You won't have to dig for diamonds

But handle me with care : I am precious

What's sure

To the test of pressure

My love came out raw, clean and pure

I've had enough of feeling blue

Imma gleam in your life like a Sapphire

UNSENT TEXTS (INTERLUDE)

I'm not trying
To own
You
I'm willing
To grow
With you

IN HALF OR IN FULL ?
(INTERLUDE)

Through my different moods
And under different moons,
Will you love me
In half or in full?

BRB

Check your compass
Your arrow is still
Pointing at me
I'm just that magnetic
I give you
That bomb personality
A bit of magic
A pinch of sass
Plus peace of mind

Your dearest friend
And your safe haven

I got the juice and the drip
Your morning cup of tea
Hot and steaming
Your dose of Oxytocin
Like coffee in the morning
I give you energy
Trust me
You'll need more than a sip

Strong, sweet, unrefined
Robust, gentle and mild
You're good for me baby
You know how to handle my wild
And you can take the spices

Your sweet dark brown sugar
Blends and marries so well
With my honey
Caramel skin
Now your love stuck
All over my body
Like maple syrup
And light molasses

You'll be right back
Just like a boomerang
I know that for a fact
Swimming ashore
To rest on my sea strands
And I'll welcome you once more

Mayeena Rose

NATURAL SATELLITES

I'm your catalyst
Even when
you try to resist
The attraction
The push and pull
Your heart remains
True and faithful
To me
Your favourite
Celestial body
And most loyal
Companion

I will reflect
The hues and the light
So your darkest parts
Can reveal their spark
Your course is perfect
Orbiting me
In safety
No crash no wreckage
No abrupt damage

But nevermind

The gravity
I'd rather fall
For you my love
Over and over
Again
I'm yours
You're mine
I think that's what
We are
Natural satellites

Mayeena Rose

LOTUS GRAND EXIT

For sure
I need you here
I want you here
But when there's no more us
Like a misty rose lotus
Delicate majestic flower
I'll survive and thrive
Without your water
Knee deep in the mud
You will see me prosper
Let me follow the stream
That was meant for me
No need
To worry
I will rebloom
In serenity

I LOVED A MAN

I met a man
and
oh...
how humanising
was it....

he was
delicately soaked in
an enlivening
super lifting
masculinity

he was verily
worthy

surely
he was a king
robust in integrity

our gathering
magnified
my feminine
energy

our words blended
songfully

in verity

beautifully imperfect
he showed virtue
and accepted
my dimmest
aspects

he gently
held my hand
while I unlearned
corrupted patterns

His fragrance
very personal
amatory
hardly waned
from my memory

capable and
respectable
He earned his seat
at my table

When it's all
said and done
standing proud
in my queendom
I can now proclaim

I know how it feels
To love a man

CHAPTER 7

UNINVITED

My elegance

Doesn't need

An audience

There's no one for me

To impress

But Myself

This is not a show

Not a public catwalk

For your visual

Pleasure

Or to feed

Your desire

As a matter of fact

Your approval

Remains stagnant

At the lowest rank

of my list of concerns

Oh

And

This was

A public service

Announcement

JUST LIKE YOU

I have been an example
Of both fragility
And fierceness
In this eventful quest
For that type of love,
That real love,
Like, unseen before.

I failed majestically.

And just like you,
I'm floating through
Waves of emotions.
I feel it in my spirit.
I feel it in my womb.
Both mourning
The fights and the babies,
The crimes and the treacheries,
The silent good-byes
And spiritual concoctions,
Flying, stinging
Like million lullabies
And jittery honeybees.

And just like you,
When I can't feel the sun
And pain can't be undone,
I dive back to my roots,
Draw the energy that's left
Deep within my core,
To radiate like full moon.
Surrounded by darkness
In a hazy winter night,
I keep my hopes
Shining bright.

DECADES
(INTERLUDE)

Bear with me
I'm recovering...

Not from the past week
Not from twenty twenty,

But from the past
Twenty-five
Years.

I'm recollecting
All the pieces of me.

It took me
Nearly
three decades to get there.

HEEDING THE NIGHT

Instead

Of being scared

Shootings stars

Compelled me

To heed the night

They were

Glaring streaks of light

Benevolent enough

To help me

Redirect my course

Feels like

When I pick-up

One of my

Favourite books

I find

My way up

Powered up

And prepared

To write my own story

With the precision

And the artistry

Of Queen Toni Morrison

I was scared of the night

Until I realised

That when you get a grasp

Of your purpose

And your craft

The darkness

becomes not

So troublesome

After all

A MOTHER (INTERLUDE)

I knew I needed you

If I wanted to find the truth

So I've been looking for you

In my eyes and in my skin tone

In my curls and in my cheekbones

And finally, we came together

When I became a mother

THE BIRTH OF A STAR

Don't you know,

It takes

Time,

A lot of time.

Stifling coldness

And dark clouds.

Unforeseen heat

And outside pressure,

Persistent and ardent

Shock waves.

Now your heart

Trembles,

I know babe,

You were almost

Blown away

In you prime.

You grew under dark clouds

But now

You're a hot shot

Capable and bright

And I know deep in your heart

Shines a huge amount of light

And since most new stars

Are created in clusters

Hold my hand,

Let's walk together.

Don't you know

It's now your time

To shine.

CULMINATION

My most beautiful

Personal

Intimate

Loving

Revolutionary act!

The highest ,

The greatest point in my life...

Oh what a ride it was...

Until your arrival

The ascension was

Laborious

Super

Extra ordinary...

And in a Whisper

It was Declared:

I would be your mother.

What a mystical event!

Such a spiritual elevation!

Grand Awakening,

Great Rising...

God, I see your Grandeur

And my whole life sings your Song!

For you I'll rearrange it

With the best harmonies ...

See, my dear son,

Here is your rightful place

In the symphony of life.

I dreamed your presence,

Envisioned your existence...

I have planned it for so long,

Your breath of life...

What a miracle

You are....

Mayeena Rose

EVENING PRAYERS

I'm aligning my soul

With the suns,

The stars and the moons.

All of us

Intentionally

Created.

And we all

Worship You

In wonderment.

The stars,

Most unyielding,

Are glancing at us

Astounded

By our deeds.

It's a heavy

Responsibility

The gift of free will.

Roaming in turmoil

I'm never wary,

Never hopeless

Of your Grace.

Instead I pray

I pray real deep

To remain immersed

In unwavering faith.

Because Your love

Is what's Above

Paramount

And tenfold.

Accompany me

In Love

Down the line,

Surround me

In Love

On the other side,

Lord of Mercy.

WALK WITH ME

I weep secretly, frequently,

And alone, I ponder in wonder,

About infinity...

About life, right here...

The mysteries and necessities

Of shattered realities.

Tell me...

Do you believe in Destiny?

And even if

We don't agree,

Will you walk with me ?

SOLTICE (INTERLUDE)

Surely the solstice

Can bring us peace

And respite...

Lord of Mercy

Look at my life,

Embrace me with your Grace.

Although the pain is rife,

I want to submit

In peace.

SUNSET

I'm preparing for that sunset

I dream it soothing

Comforting

Although

I'm a bit scared

Of the unknown

My faith keeps me brave...

Among life's many surprises

I know it to be a guarantee.

I've been blessed enough

To see so many sunrises,

I've been blessed to travel

A dozen times around the sun.

I've loved, I've lived,

I've lost, I've learned.

And when I look at the stars and the moons

I know Your Love is Plentiful.

I'm preparing for that promise
That transcends all creeds.

I pray for a Day
Of Mercy and Benevolence,
An enchanting and calm
Summery nightfall.

I pray the constellations
The mountains and the angels
Plead in our favour,
I hope the stars will shine bright
And beg Mercy for our plight.

I pray they repeat the same petition
For entire generations.

Printed in Poland
by Amazon Fulfillment
Poland Sp. z o.o., Wrocław